SPOTLIGHT ON SPACE SCIENCE

JOURNEY TO JUPITER

GREG P. CUNNINGHAM

PowerKiDS press.
New York

South Huntington Public Library
145 Pidgeon Hill Road
Huntington Station, NY 11746

Published in 2015 by The Rosen Publishing Group, Inc.
29 East 21st Street, New York, NY 10010

Copyright © 2015 by The Rosen Publishing Group, Inc.

All rights reserved. No part of this book may be reproduced in any form without permission in writing from the publisher, except by a reviewer.

First Edition

Editor: Susan Meyer
Book Design: Kris Everson

Photo Credits: Cover (main), pp. 9, 19, 27 NASA/JPL; cover (planet Jupiter) NASA/JPL/University of Arizona; p. 5 NASA/The Hubble Heritage Team, STScI, AURA, Amy Simon Cornell; p. 7 Neo Edmund/Shutterstock.com; p. 11 ESA/Herschel/T. Cavalié et al.; NASA/ESA/Reta Beebe (New Mexico State University); pp. 13, 15, 23, 24, 25 NASA; p. 17 NASA/ESA/K. Retherford/SWRI; p. 18 NASA/JPL-Caltech/University of Arizona; p. 21 NASA, ESA, and E. Karkoschka (University of Arizona); p. 29 NASA/JPL-Caltech.

Library of Congress Cataloging-in-Publication Data

Cunningham, Greg.
Journey to Jupiter / by Greg Cunningham.
p. cm. — (Spotlight on space science)
Includes index.
ISBN 978-1-4994-0370-1 (pbk.)
ISBN 978-1-4994-0399-2 (6-pack)
ISBN 978-1-4994-0416-6 (library binding)
1. Jupiter (Planet) — Juvenile literature. 2. Jupiter (Planet) — Exploration — Juvenile literature. I. Title.
QB661.C86 2015
523.45—d23

Manufactured in the United States of America

CPSIA Compliance Information: Batch #CW15PK: For Further Information contact Rosen Publishing, New York, New York at 1-800-237-9932

CONTENTS

A GIANT AMONG PLANETS....................4
FROM GAS AND DUST......................6
JUPITER'S ORBIT........................8
THE LAYERS OF JUPITER..................10
COLORFUL SWIRLS AND STORMS.............12
MOONS OF JUPITER......................14
THE LARGEST MOONS.....................16
THE VOLCANIC MOON.....................18
EARLY ASTRONOMERS.....................20
STUDYING JUPITER......................22
JUPITER'S GIANT RINGS.................24
THE *GALILEO* PROBE...................26
THE FUTURE OF JUPITER EXPLORATION.....28
GLOSSARY..............................30
FOR MORE INFORMATION..................31
INDEX.................................32

A GIANT AMONG PLANETS
CHAPTER 1

Jupiter is the fifth **planet** from the Sun and the most massive planet in the **solar system**.

It's impossible to comprehend the size of our own planet, but Jupiter's enormous size is truly mind-blowing. If you could drive a car at 60 miles per hour (97 km/h), day and night without stopping, it would take just over two weeks to drive around Earth's **equator**. To drive around giant Jupiter, however, would take six months! In fact, if Earth's diameter is compared to Jupiter's, the giant planet has a diameter that's 11 times the size of Earth's.

Jupiter is hundreds of millions of miles (km) from Earth. It is so large, though, that it is actually possible to see Jupiter without a telescope. This means the earliest humans would have looked up into the night sky and been able to see the king of the planets shining brightly.

This photo of Jupiter was captured by the Hubble Space Telescope in 2010.

FROM GAS AND DUST
CHAPTER 2

About five billion years ago, Jupiter, Earth, the other six planets in the solar system, and even the Sun did not exist.

The chemical ingredients to make the Sun and everything in our solar system did exist, however. These ingredients were floating in space in a vast cloud of gas and dust called a **nebula**.

Over millions of years, part of the cloud began to collapse on itself, forming a massive rotating sphere, or ball. A disk formed around the sphere from the remaining gas and dust. The material in the sphere was pressed together by **gravity**, causing it to heat up and pressure to build. Eventually, the heat and pressure became so great that the sphere ignited and became a star. This new star was our Sun.

Gas and dust continued to spin in a disk around the newly formed star. Over time, material in the disk clumped together to form four rocky planets and four planets made mostly of gas, plus the **moons**, **asteroids**, and every other object in the solar system.

The rotating mass of matter around a star from which planets are formed is called a protoplanetary disk. "Proto" comes from the Greek word meaning "first" or "before."

JUPITER'S ORBIT
CHAPTER 3

Like every object in the solar system, Jupiter **orbits** the Sun. As it makes its journey around the Sun, it is traveling through space at just over 29,000 miles per hour (47,000 km/h).

Earth orbits the Sun once every 365 days, a time period we call a year. Jupiter is much further from the Sun, however, so it takes 4,333 days to make one full orbit. So a year on Jupiter lasts nearly 12 years! In that time, Jupiter makes a journey of 3,037,011,311 miles (4,887,595,931 km).

As the planets in the solar system orbit the Sun, each one also rotates, or spins, on its **axis**. Earth rotates once every 24 hours. Jupiter spins much faster than Earth, though, and takes just under 10 hours to make one full rotation.

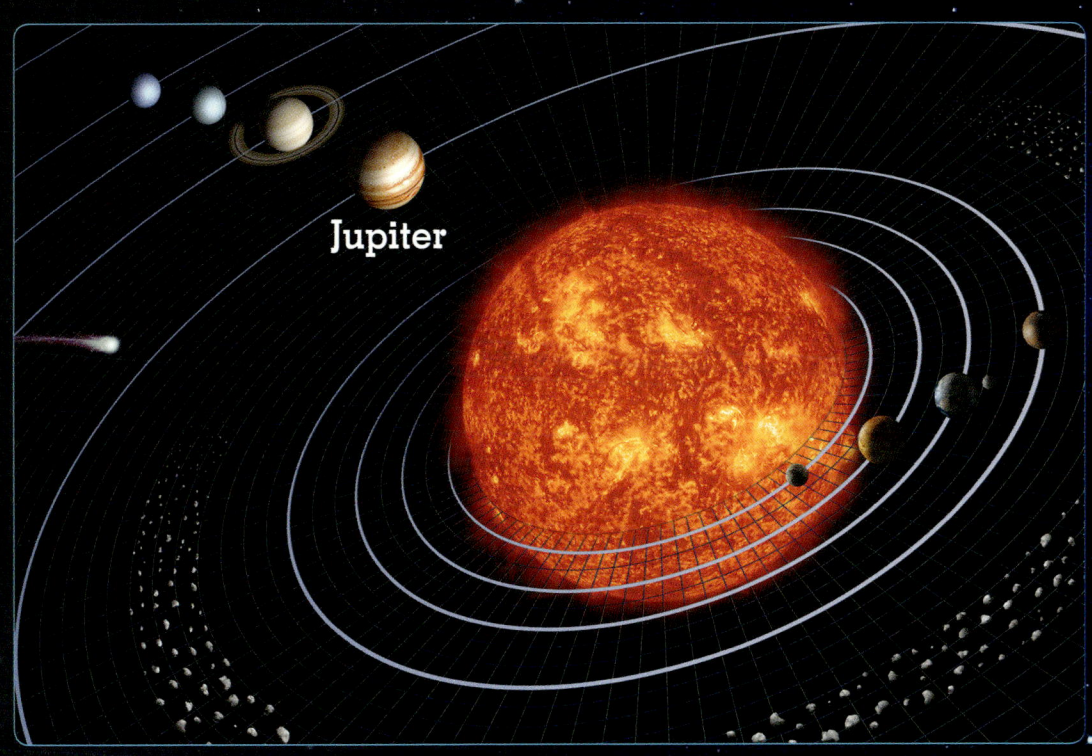

Here the planets are not drawn to scale, but are in their correct order. Jupiter is the fifth farthest planet from the Sun.

THE LAYERS OF JUPITER
CHAPTER 4

Unlike the planet where we live, Jupiter has no outer solid surface. The planet is a massive ball of gases and liquids.

Jupiter is surrounded by a colorful layer of clouds. Below the clouds is a layer of hydrogen and helium gas that is 600 miles (1,000 km) thick. This gaseous layer is the planet's **atmosphere**.

Beneath the atmosphere is a layer made up of liquid hydrogen, which is about 12,500 miles (20,000 km) deep. Deeper into the planet, the pressure is so great that the liquid hydrogen actually becomes metallic, forming a layer that is 25,000 miles (40,000 km) deep. In the very center of the planet, scientists believe there may be a solid rocky core that is slightly larger than Earth.

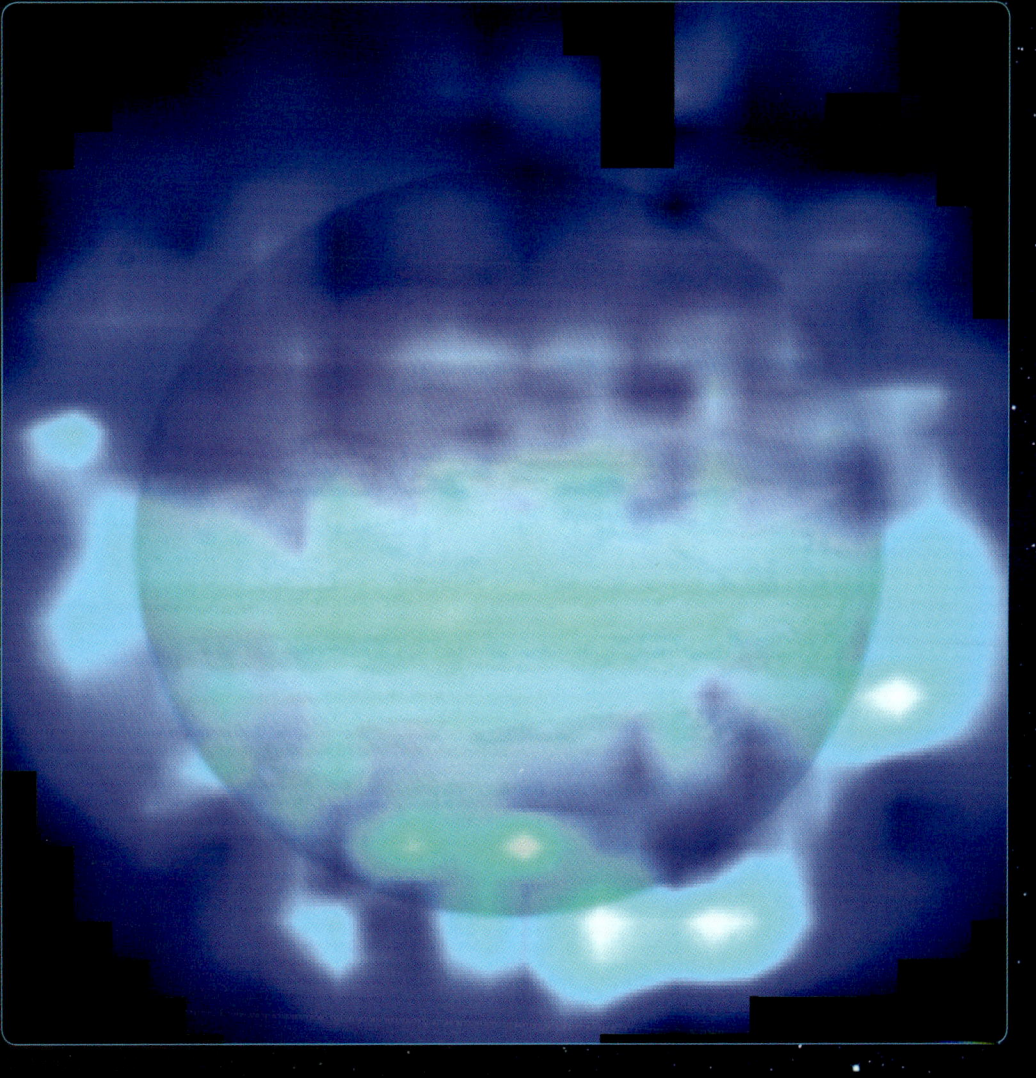

In addition to hydrogen and helium, scientists now know that Jupiter's atmosphere also contains water. This photo shows the concentration of water. The light blue shows where water levels are the highest.

COLORFUL SWIRLS AND STORMS
CHAPTER 5

When we look at Jupiter through a telescope, we see swirling white, orange, brown, and red clouds.

The layer of clouds surrounding Jupiter is about 30 miles (48 km) thick. The clouds are made mostly of the gas ammonia, with small quantities of **water vapor**, crystals of ice, and other **elements**.

Jupiter's best-known feature that can be seen through a telescope is a giant spinning storm called the Great Red Spot. This storm can be compared to a hurricane on Earth, but it is much larger than any hurricane on our planet. The vast oval-shaped storm has gotten smaller over time. In 2014, scientists measured it at its smallest size yet: a still huge 10,250 miles (16,494 km) across! Inside the Great Red Spot, swirling winds reach speeds of about 270 miles per hour (434 km/h).

The Great Red Spot was first spotted hundreds of years ago. The storm is still around, but it has gotten smaller over the years.

MOONS OF JUPITER
CHAPTER 6

A moon is a rocky object that orbits a planet. Mercury has no moons, Earth has just one, while Mars has two. Jupiter, however, may have over 60 moons!

Jupiter's giant size means its gravity is very powerful. Over the billions of years of its life, it has pulled many rocky space objects into orbit around it.

The number of moons orbiting Jupiter is not definite, because when a new moon is discovered orbiting a planet, astronomers need to watch and track it for some time. Once they are sure the moon is permanently orbiting the planet and is not just a rocky object temporarily passing the planet, the moon is named and becomes official. At the end of 2014, Jupiter had 50 confirmed, permanent moons. There are 16 other possible moons being watched and studied.

Jupiter's four largest moons are named Ganymede, Callisto, Europa, and Io. Ganymede is the largest moon in the solar system.

Jupiter's moons were first photographed by Voyager 1. Here they are seen, not to scale, but in their correct relative positions. Io is in the upper left, Europa is in the center by Jupiter, and in the lower right are Ganymede and Callisto.

15

THE LARGEST MOONS
CHAPTER 7

Jupiter's giant moon Ganymede is covered by a thick outer shell of ice, which may be as thick as 497 miles (800 km).

Long grooves and ridges have formed in Ganymede's icy crust. Some of the ridges run for thousands of miles (km) and can be as high as mountains here on Earth.

Over time, the surfaces of most planets and moons change. This happens when superhot, liquid rock, called **lava**, spills onto the surface through cracks or **volcanoes**. The lava cools and hardens, forming rocks, changing the look of the land, and filling in craters formed when asteroids and other space objects crash into the surface of a planet or moon.

Jupiter's moon Callisto has not had this hot underground activity, however. With no lava to reshape the landscape, four billion years of impacts with other space bodies have left the moon's surface covered in craters.

Europa is covered by a giant frozen ocean, but scientists believe there might be liquid water beneath the frozen crust. This artist's illustration shows what a plume of water shooting forth from Europa might look like.

THE VOLCANIC MOON
CHAPTER 8

Jupiter's moon Io has an ever-changing landscape because it is the most volcanically active body in the solar system.

As Io orbits Jupiter, the huge planet's gravity pulls at the little moon. This has a dramatic effect on the moon's surface.

If you've ever spent a day at the beach, you have seen how the ocean's water level rises and falls. This change in water levels, called the tide, is actually caused by the Moon's gravity pulling Earth's water toward it. A similar effect happens on Io, except that Io has no oceans. That means Jupiter's gravity actually pulls at the rocky surface of Io, causing it to bulge up and down.

Volcanic activity is common on Io, as seen in this photo of a lava filled crater, taken by the *Galileo* craft.

This pulling and stretching of Io's surface causes tremendous heat to build up, so there is always superhot, liquid rock below the moon's crust. As Io's surface bulges and stretches, lava from below the crust bursts onto the surface through cracks and volcanoes.

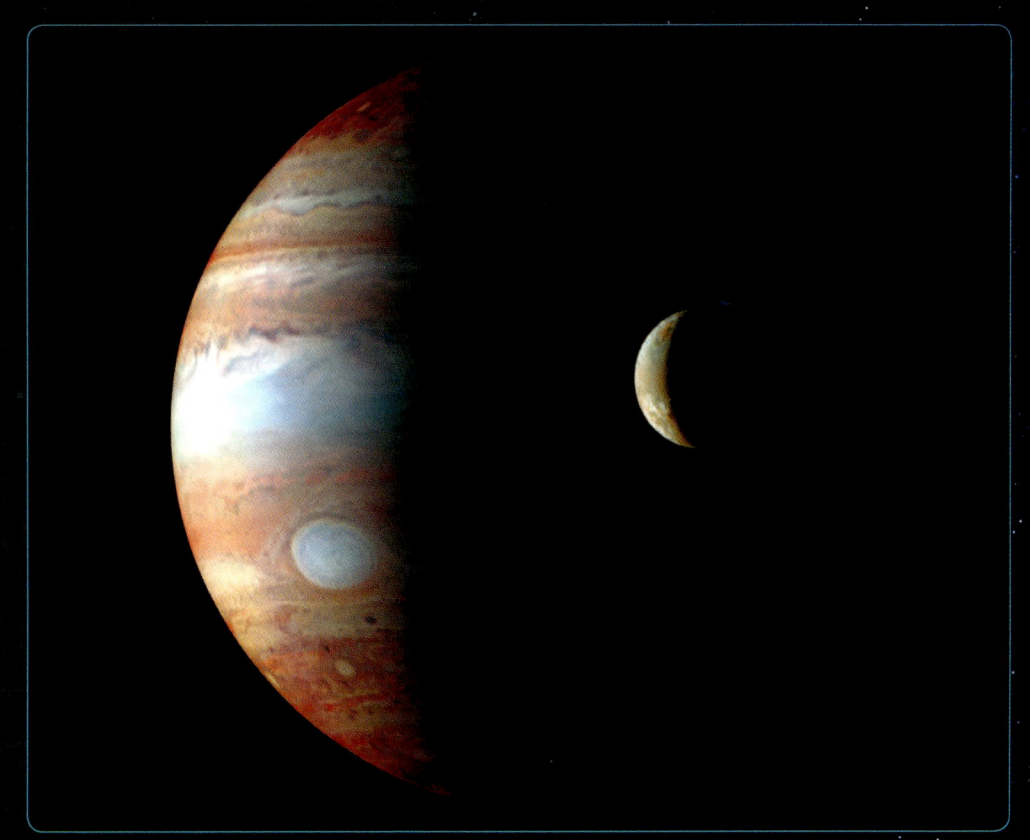

With over 400 active volcanoes, Io is the most volcanically active moon in the solar system.

EARLY ASTRONOMERS
CHAPTER 9

For around 4.5 billion years, the planets in our solar system have been orbiting the Sun, each taking its own path, or orbit, around our star.

Early astronomers with no telescopes or other equipment saw the planets as distant points of light. Ancient Greek astronomers noticed how the points of light moved in the night sky and named them *planetes*, which means "wanderers."

The ancient Romans also observed the planets Mercury, Venus, Mars, Jupiter, and Saturn. They named these bright objects after their gods. Jupiter was named after the king of the Roman gods.

When the telescope was invented in the early 1600s, astronomers were able to study the planets in more detail. One of these stargazers was the Italian astronomer Galileo Galilei.

In 1610, Galileo discovered what he at first thought were four stars near Jupiter. He had, in fact, discovered Jupiter's four largest moons, Ganymede, Callisto, Io, and Europa.

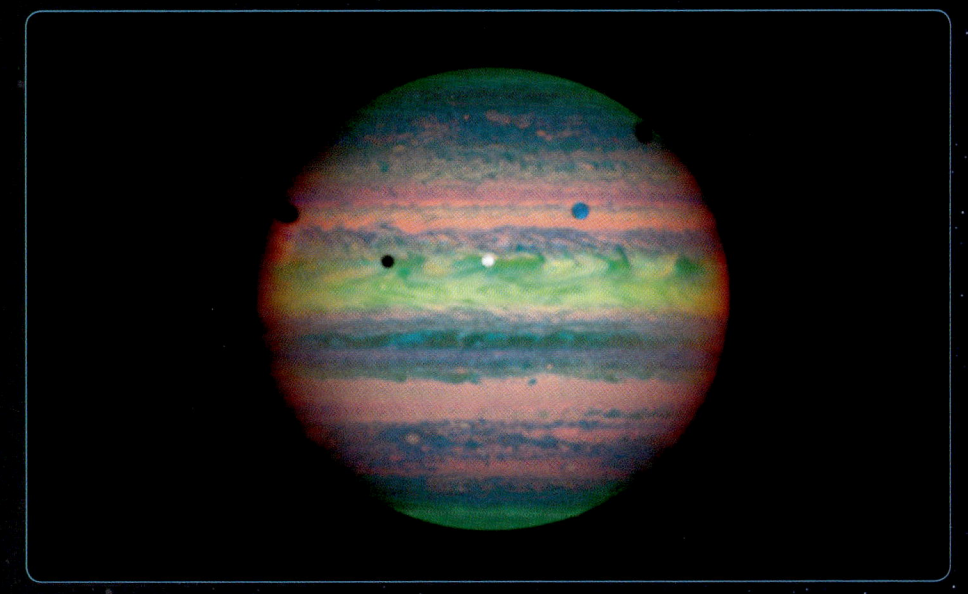

This Hubble Space Telescope photo shows two of Jupiter's four moons in front of the planet. Io is the small white dot and Ganymede is the blue dot. Their shadows, and the shadow of a third moon Callisto, can also be seen.

STUDYING JUPITER
CHAPTER 10

For hundreds of years, astronomers studied Jupiter through telescopes. Then, in March 1972, a spacecraft named *Pioneer 10* left Earth on a mission to study Jupiter.

As *Pioneer 10* flew past Jupiter, it transmitted hundreds of photos of the planet and its moons back to Earth. In December 1974, on its way to study Saturn, *Pioneer 11* also flew past Jupiter. Flying at 26,570 miles (42,760 km) above Jupiter's clouds, *Pioneer 11* captured the first ever pictures of Jupiter's polar regions.

In late summer 1977, *Voyager 1* and *Voyager 2* blasted off from Earth. Part of their missions was to study Jupiter as they passed the planet on their way to the outer reaches of the solar system. *Voyager 1* captured images of Ganymede, Callisto, Europa, and Io. This allowed astronomers to see the surfaces of these moons for the first time. *Voyager 1* also discovered that Io is home to many active volcanoes.

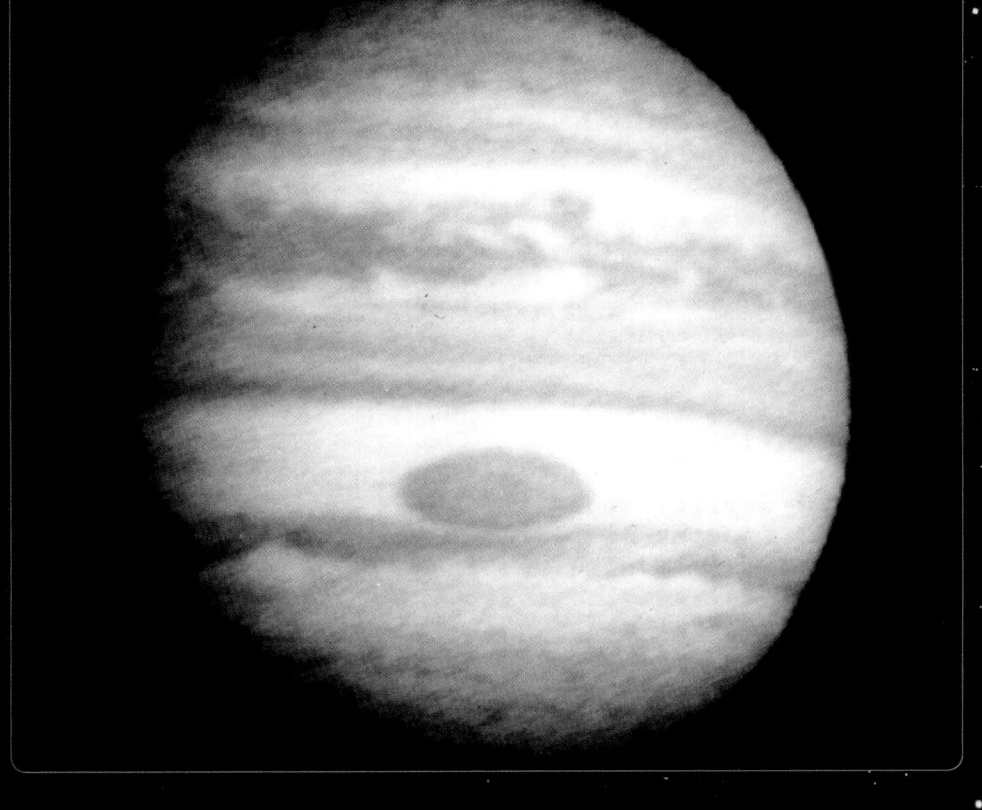

Jupiter was photographed by Pioneer 10 *in December 1973 from a distance of 1,842,451 miles (2,695,000 km).*

JUPITER'S GIANT RINGS
CHAPTER 11

When the two *Voyager* spacecraft visited Jupiter in 1979, they captured images showing that Jupiter is surrounded by rings that are made up of dust and tiny pieces of rock.

There is one main ring encircling the planet that is about 4,300 miles (7,000 km) wide. Two of Jupiter's smaller moons, Adrastea and Metis, are orbiting Jupiter inside this ring. Scientists think that some of the rock and dust in the ring could be rubble created when other space bodies collided with the two moons.

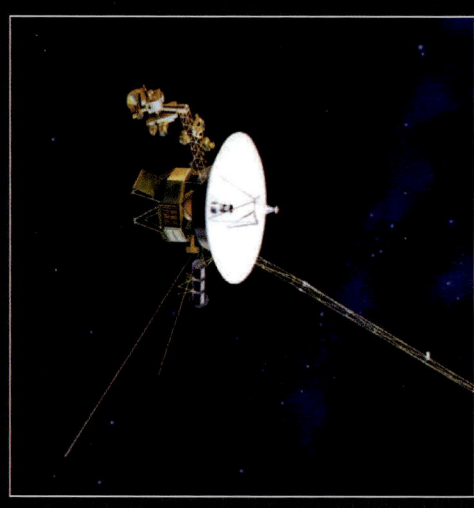

artwork of a *Voyager* spacecraft

On the inner edge of the main ring is the Halo. This ring is about 12,400 miles (20,000 km) thick.

24

On the outer edge of the main ring is a ring of dust particles that are so small they would look no thicker than smoke. This outer ring is about 52,800 miles (85,000 km) wide.

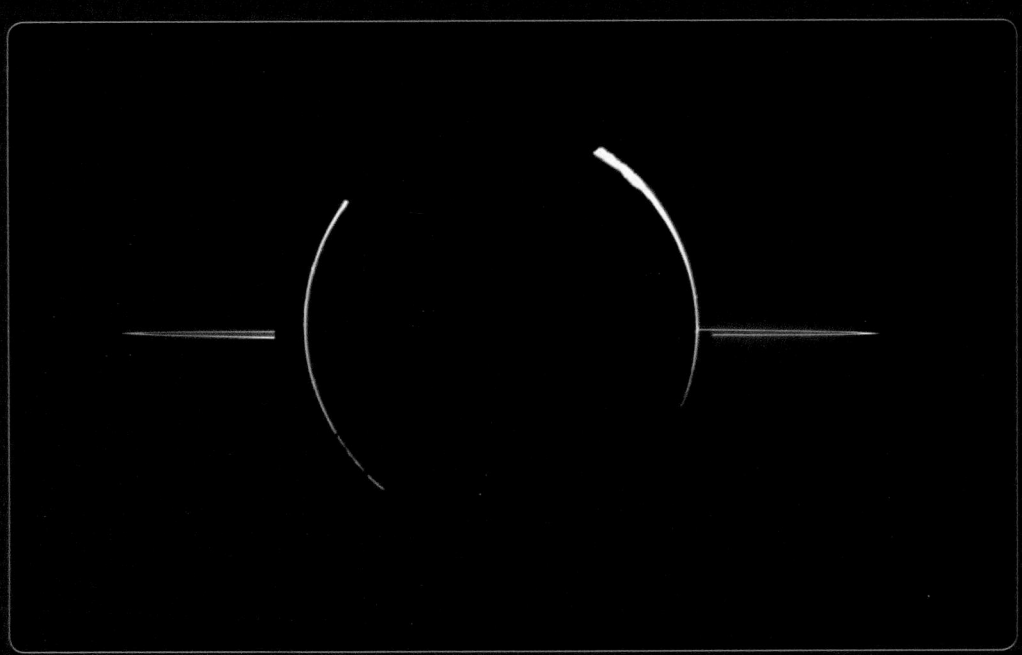

When Jupiter eclipsed the Sun, the Galileo spacecraft was able to take this photo. The sunlight illuminates the dust that forms rings around the planet.

THE *GALILEO* PROBE
CHAPTER 12

In October 1989, the NASA spacecraft *Galileo* was launched. Named for the astronomer who discovered Jupiter's largest moons, *Galileo* was carried into space aboard the space shuttle *Atlantis*.

In July 1995, when *Galileo* was still about 50 million miles (80 million km) from Jupiter, it released a probe that plunged into Jupiter's atmosphere. The probe examined Jupiter's clouds and studied the temperature, pressure, and chemical composition of Jupiter's atmosphere. The *Galileo* probe transmitted data back to the spacecraft for 58 minutes before it was crushed, melted, or vaporized by the extreme conditions in the gas giant's atmosphere.

In December 1995, *Galileo* entered Jupiter's orbit and began its study of the planet and its moons, which would last for nearly eight years. In that time, *Galileo* detected a belt of radiation above

Jupiter's clouds and discovered that Jupiter has similar amounts of helium in its atmosphere as the Sun. It also found evidence that below Europa's icy surface there might be liquid water.

Galileo's probe descended into Jupiter's atmosphere and sent back data to the Galileo orbiter. These data transmissions are represented by blue dots in this artist's interpretation.

THE FUTURE OF JUPITER EXPLORATION
CHAPTER 13

As you read this book, NASA's *Juno* spacecraft is hurtling through space toward Jupiter. *Juno* launched in August 2011, and it will enter into orbit around Jupiter in July 2016. During its planned one-year mission, *Juno* will orbit Jupiter 33 times. Even though Jupiter is hundreds of millions of miles (km) from the Sun, *Juno's* power will be provided by **solar panels** that will capture the Sun's energy.

Even though astronomers have been studying Jupiter for centuries, this faraway planet, hidden behind miles (km) of thick clouds, still holds many mysteries. Instruments aboard *Juno* will allow astronomers to see below Jupiter's thick clouds for the first time. *Juno* will study the gas giant's atmosphere and internal layers.

It will also study how the gas giant formed. Studying Jupiter's formation will not only give scientists information about this planet, but will help answer many questions about how our entire solar system formed.

Juno *is planned to begin orbiting Jupiter in 2016. It will observe the clouds of Jupiter from as close as 3,100 miles (5,000 km) away.*

GLOSSARY

asteroid: A small, rocky, planet-like body in space that circles the Sun.

atmosphere: The gases that surround a planet.

axis: An imaginary line through the center of an object, around which the object rotates.

element: A part of something.

equator: An imaginary circle that divides a planet into two equal parts.

gravity: The attraction of the mass of a body in space for other bodies nearby.

lava: Liquid rock that flows from a hole in a planet's surface.

moon: A natural object that circles a planet.

nebula: A huge cloud of dust and gas found between stars.

orbit: To travel in a circle or oval around something.

planet: A large body in space that has its own orbit around the Sun or another star.

solar panel: A panel of cells that change energy from the Sun into electricity.

solar system: The Sun and the space bodies that move around it, including the planets and their moons.

volcano: An opening in a planet's crust that lets out hot, liquid rock.

water vapor: Water in the form of gas.

FOR MORE INFORMATION

BOOKS

Aguilar, David A. *Space Encyclopedia: A Tour of Our Solar System and Beyond.* Washington, D.C.: National Geographic, 2013.

Carson, Mary Kay. *Far-Out Guide to Jupiter.* Berkeley Heights, NJ: Enslow, 2011.

Squire, Ann O. *Planet Jupiter.* New York, NY: Children's Press, 2014.

WEBSITES

Due to the changing nature of Internet links, PowerKids Press has developed an online list of websites related to the subject of this book. This site is updated regularly. Please use this link to access the list: www.powerkidslinks.com/soss/jupi

INDEX

A
atmosphere, 10, 11, 26, 27, 28

C
Callisto, 15, 16, 21, 22
clouds, 6, 10, 12, 22, 26, 27, 28, 29

E
Europa, 15, 17, 21, 22, 27

G
Galilei, Galileo, 20, 21
Galileo, 18, 25, 26, 27
Ganymede, 15, 16, 21, 22
gases, 6, 7, 10, 12
gas giant, 26, 28, 29
gravity, 6, 14, 18
Great Red Spot, 12, 13

H
helium, 10, 11, 27
hydrogen, 10, 11

I
Io, 15, 18, 19, 21, 22

J
Juno, 28, 29

M
moons, 7, 14, 15, 16, 18, 19, 21, 22, 23, 24, 26

N
nebula, 6

P
Pioneer 10, 22, 23
Pioneer 11, 22

R
rings, 24, 25

S
solar system, 4, 6, 7, 8, 15, 18, 19, 20, 22, 29

V
volcanoes, 16, 18, 19, 23
Voyager 1, 15, 22, 23, 24
Voyager 2, 22, 24

W
water, 11, 12, 17, 18, 27